AZTECS, INCAS AND MAYANS FOR CHILDREN

ANCIENT CIVILIZATIONS FOR KIDS 4TH GRADE CHILDREN'S ANCIENT HISTORY

Speedy Publishing LLC
40 E. Main St. #1156
Newark, DE 19711
www.speedypublishing.com
Copyright 2017

All Rights reserved. No part of this book may be reproduced or used in any way or form or by any means whether electronic or mechanical, this means that you cannot record or photocopy any material ideas or tips that are provided in this book.

In this book, we're going to talk about the Mayans, Incas, and Aztecs. So, let's get right to it!

Before the Europeans came to the Americas, there were three very advanced civilizations of native people already living there. The Mayan civilization was first, followed by the Incas and Aztecs.

INCA RUINS

These three civilizations dominated the area that today we call Mesoamerica. This region extends from the central section of Mexico to Guatemala and Belize. It continues through Honduras and El Salvador as well.

MAYAN RUINS

THE MAYAN CIVILIZATION

It's believed that the Mayans began their civilization around 2000 BC. In Mesoamerica, they had a dominant presence for more than 3000 years until explorers from Spain came there in 1519 AD. The Mayan people were farmers.

They lived on the Yucatan Peninsula and their civilization expanded to the surrounding southern highlands. They eventually spread out from those locations to the northern section of El Salvador. The region was an area that had a large amount of volcanic activity, which made the soil very fertile for growing crops.

MAYAN CITY OF PALENQUE

From 250 to 900 AD, which was considered their golden age, they constructed settlements that were organized as city-states. Throughout the course of their long history, various city-states were the centers of power at different times.

The city-states of El Mirador as well as Tikal, Caracol, and perhaps the most famous, Chichen Itza, were the most important settlements at different times.

The Mayan people were excellent builders. Today, they are best known for their tall pyramids with stepped-up sides that extended high above the jungle trees. The limestone quarries in the area provided all the stone they needed.

They also organized their buildings arranged as public plazas. The enormous columns were inscribed with information recording their history.

Archaeologists have been excavating at Tikal in Guatemala for many decades. At one time it was one of the oldest of the Mayan settlements. Thousands of artifacts and architectural wonders have been excavated at Tikal. The discoveries include ornate temples, step pyramids, and courts where ball games were played. Monuments carved in stone, everyday tools, objects used during religious ceremonies, and fragments of pottery have also been found. All these buildings and artifacts give us a detailed understanding of the ancient Mayan civilization.

THE INCAN CIVILIZATION

Around 1200 AD, the Incas began to settle in Peru in the Andes Mountains. At the beginning, they inhabited the Valley of Cuzco, but more than two hundred years later, between 1440 to 1500 AD, their civilization began to grow by leaps and bounds.

Eventually, their population grew to about 16 million people and they spread out over an area that spanned over 2,500 miles. The land they settled was varied and included mountainous terrain, desert regions with coastlines, and low-elevation jungles. They had to adapt to these different environmental conditions.

Their government was located at Cuzco. Their strong army kept them safe from neighboring tribes. They maintained order with laws that created standard customs as well as a standard language and a calendar. They designed and built over 14,000 miles of roadways. They also created complex bridges and tunnels. To farm in the difficult locations with mountainous terrain, they learned to build sophisticated terraces and methods of irrigation.

This type of terrace can be seen in the ancient ruins of Machu Picchu. Another example of their amazing engineering skills is Sacsahuaman, an enormous fortress built with closely fitting stones.

SACSAYHUAMÁN, CUZCO

THE FORTRESS OF SACSAHUAMAN

Sacsahuaman is located on the peak of a hill above Cuzco, the ancient Incan capital city. It is situated at an elevation of 12,000 feet. Behind the stone walls of this fortress, there were palaces, courtyards that were paved, and supply storehouses. There was an amazing water reservoir for the storage of 50,000 gallons of water. Supposedly, Sacsahuaman was built between the years 1438 AD and 1500 AD, but many believe that an earlier civilization had built it and the Incas built upon the structure that was already in existence.

Just like the pyramids in Egypt, this structure defies explanation in many ways. There are stone boulders that are 25 feet in height and 12 feet in thickness, but the stone quarries are located about 20 miles away!

No one knows how the Incas moved these massive stones across streams, down very steep ravines, and then up to the peak of the hill. The stones are amazing for another reason as well. They fit together so perfectly that a gauge to measure thickness can't be inserted between them.

FRANCISCO PIZARRO

Unfortunately, the giant fortress couldn't prevent the end of the Incan Empire. In 1533, Francisco Pizarro conquered them. They had been weakened by their own wars and the diseases the Spanish brought with them, such as smallpox.

THE AZTEC CIVILIZATION

The Valley of Mexico was the central hub of the civilization of the Aztecs. It is a huge basin high in the Sierra Madre mountain range. The temperate climate there was just right for farming. The lowlands that surrounded the area where they lived had tropical weather that was both warm and wet. Circa 1325 AD, the Aztecs decided to build on an island that was located in the middle of a lake.

THE VALLEY OF MEXICO

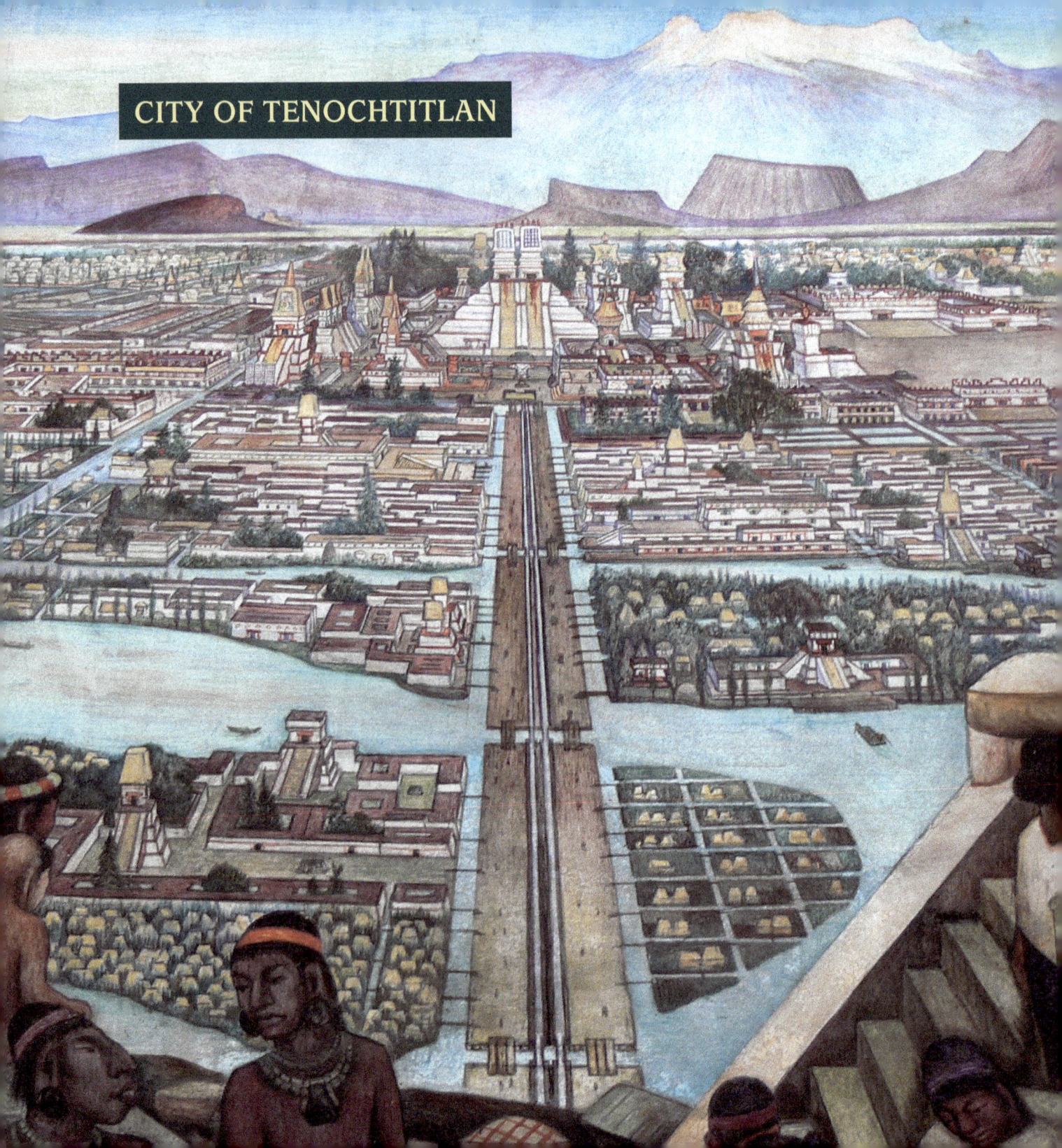

The lake was Lake Texcoco and there they built their enormous capital city called Tenochtitlán. During its golden age, the city had a population of more than 200,000. At the central hub of the city, there was a large sacred complex with pyramid temples as well as the king's palace. The city was carefully planned as if it had been drawn out on a grid with separated districts. The Aztecs built causeways so they could travel from the mainland to the island. They also constructed aqueducts to carry fresh water into the city for their people and livestock to drink.

The Aztecs, who described themselves as the Mexica, became experts at many different things. They grew massive fields of corn and were accomplished farmers. They were fierce warriors. Their aggression and skill in war helped them to protect their own civilization as well as take control over other nearby tribes. They often sacrificed their prisoners to their many gods.

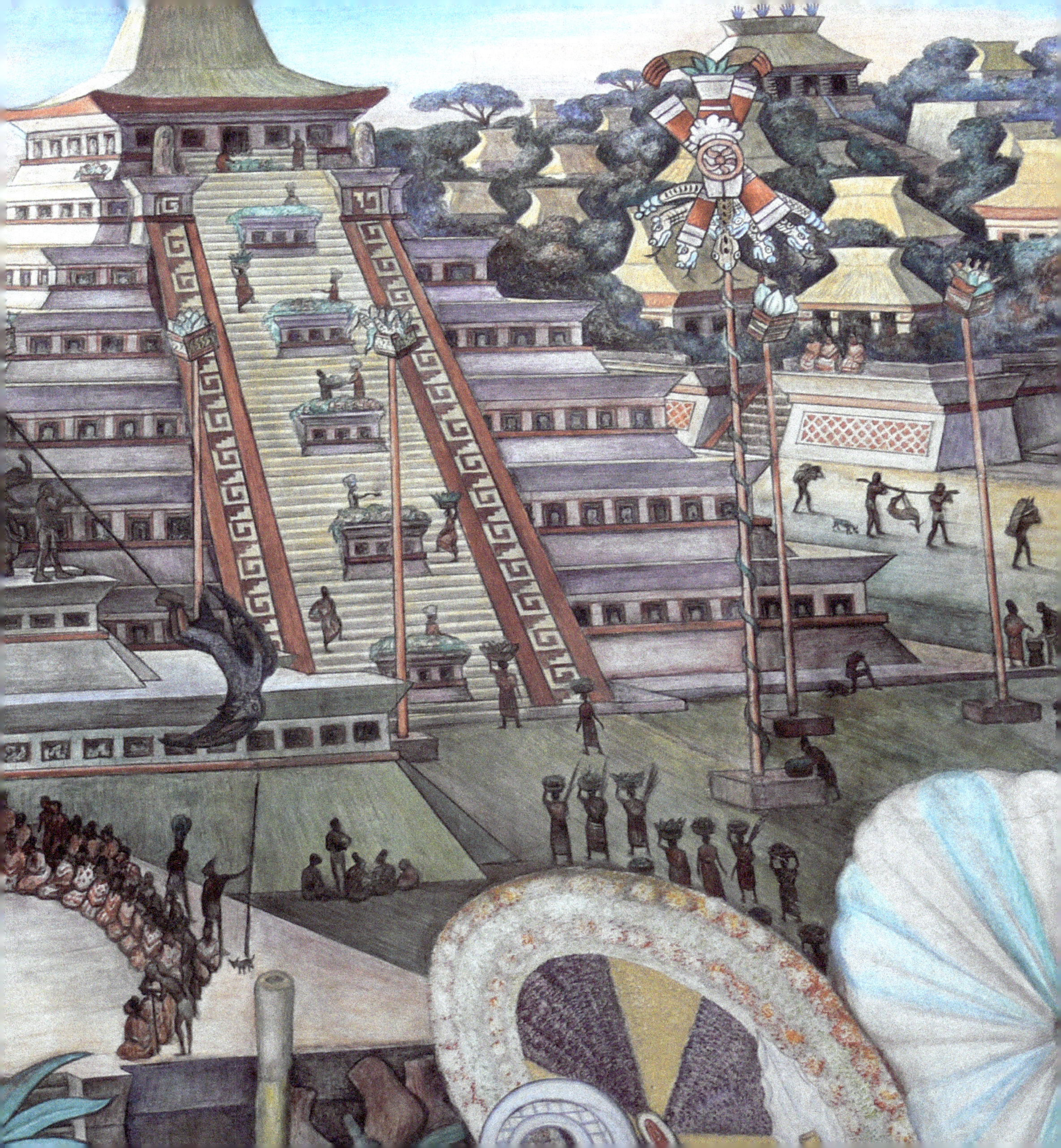

AZTECS PYRAMID

The Aztecs were also masters at designing and building temples and other structures. They built a very successful empire, which eventually reigned over the central section of what is known today as Mexico. Their civilization grew to a population numbering in the millions.

The Aztec ruler was described as the Tlatoani and during their height, Montezuma I was Tlatoani. Circa 1517 AD, the priests in the city began to envision something terrible happening. In 1519, the Spanish explorer Cortes landed in Mexico.

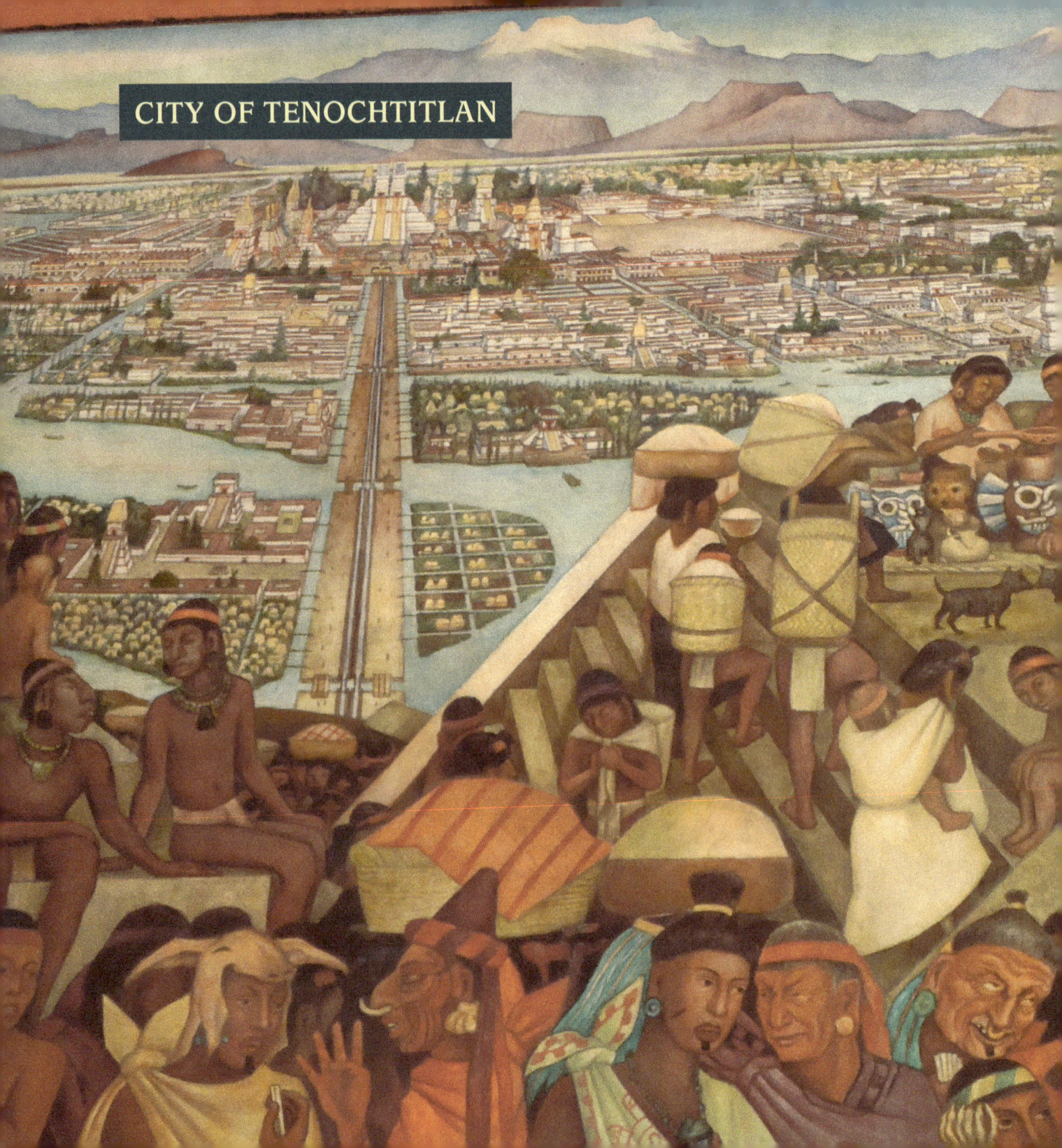

CITY OF TENOCHTITLAN

Two years later the Spanish had destroyed the beautiful Aztec city of Tenochtitlán and today one of the largest cities in the world, Mexico City, is located there.

ACCOMPLISHMENTS OF THE MAYANS, INCAS, AND AZTECS

The Mayans constructed elaborate cities. They had a sophisticated writing system that took archaeologists a long time to decode. They were the only civilization in the Americas to have a complex system for written language. They also had a system of mathematical symbols that allowed them to make a record of numbers over one million. Their knowledge of astronomy was very advanced. With this knowledge, they created two different types of calendars.

MAYAN ZODIAC CIRCLE

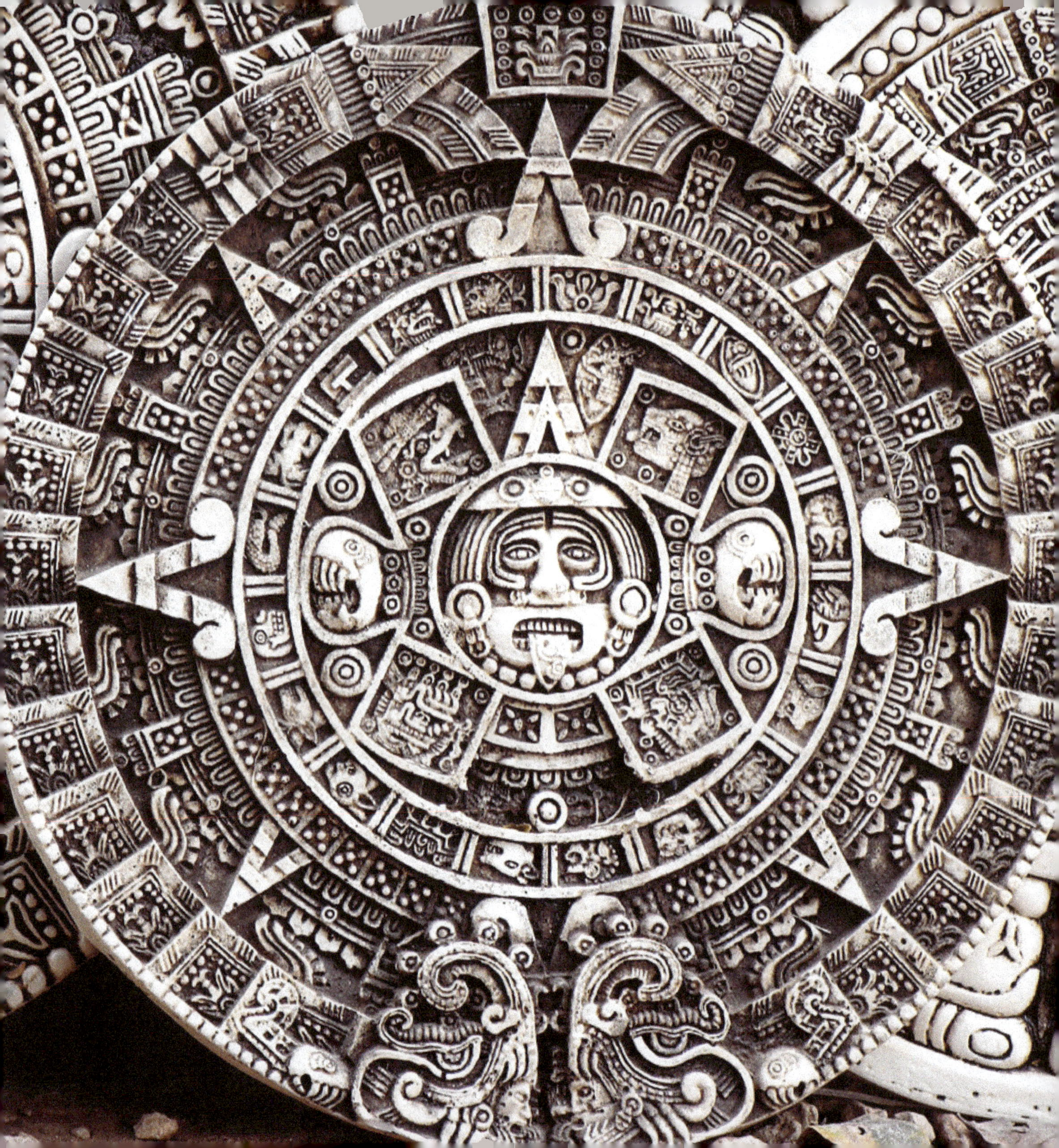

One of the calendars was designed upon the movements of the sun and earth. The other was an almanac that was based on their sacred teachings.

Although the Incas didn't have a system of writing, they were still able to enforce laws and had a central government. Their cities were carefully planned. They had terraced farms on the mountainsides. They found a way to keep inventory records with knotted cords in bundles that are today known as quipus.

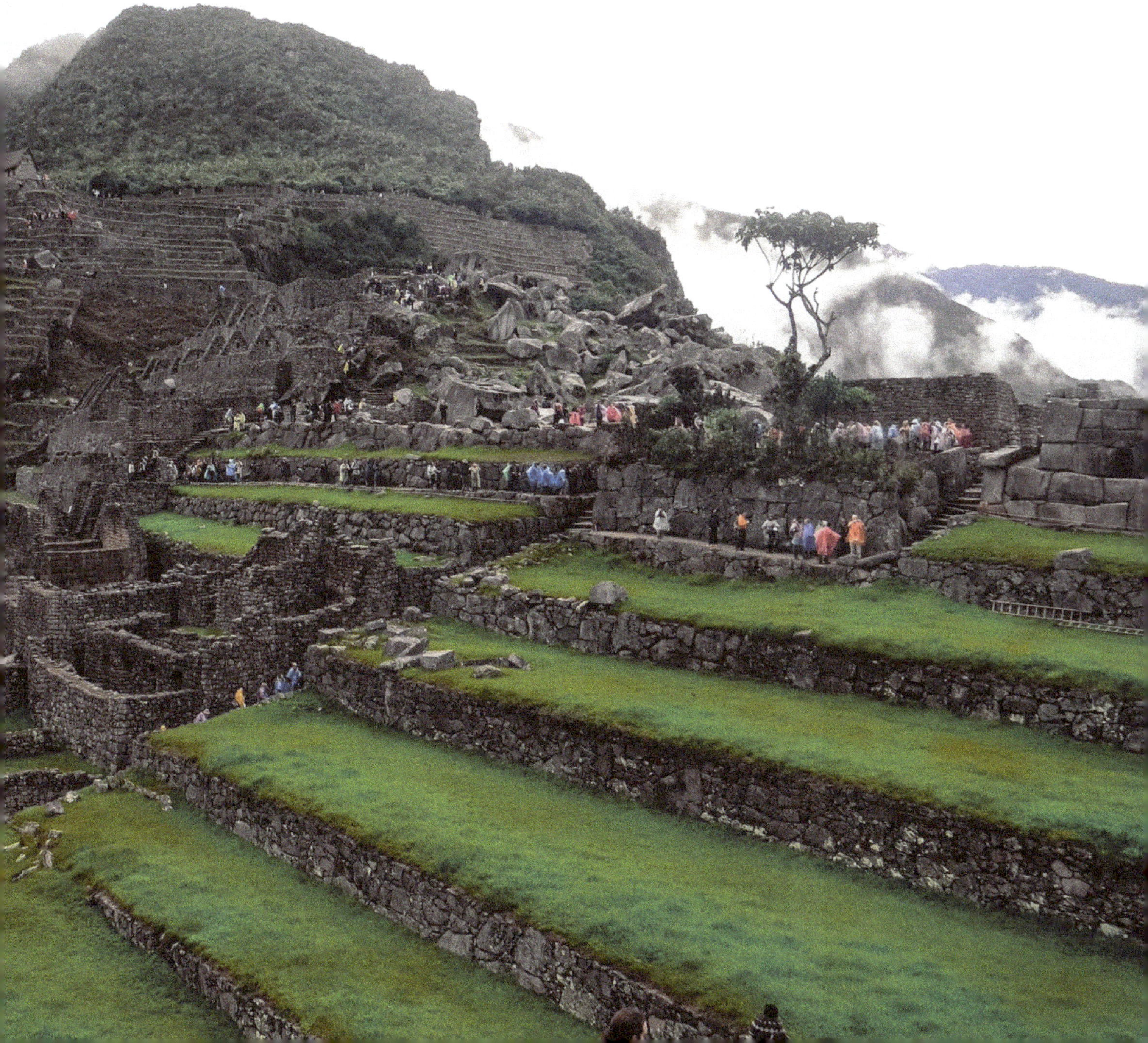

AZTEC CALENDAR

The Aztec Civilization is considered to be the greatest of these three. Like the Mayans, the Aztecs had a calendar for their religious ceremonies as well as a 365-day calendar for farming reference.

Though their writing was not as complex as the Mayan system for writing, they did have glyphs, which stood for sounds as well as words. Amazingly, a few Aztec books still remain. These books, which are known as codices, provide information about daily life in the world of the Aztecs.

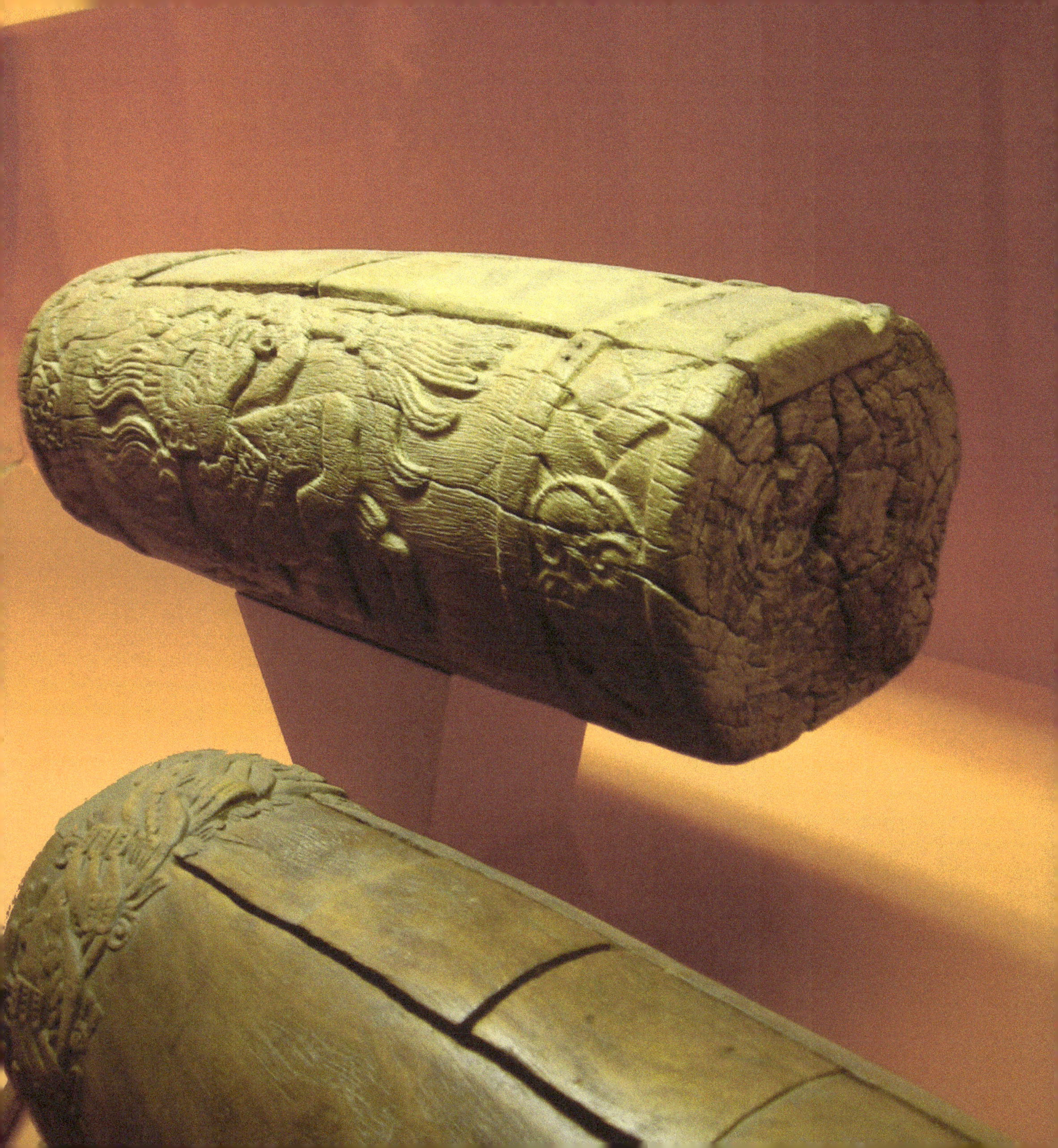

SUMMARY

Before the Europeans set foot in the Americas, there were many powerful, advanced, native civilizations.

The Mayans began their civilization on the Yucatan Peninsula and expanded to surrounding areas. They had the only complex writing system in the Americas. They had sophisticated knowledge of mathematics, astronomy, and architecture as well.

The Incas built a stone fortress with huge boulders at their capital of Cuzco. They also built thousands of miles of roads that stretched along the west coast of South America.

INCA RUINS

TENOCHTITLAN

The Aztecs built the beautiful city of Tenochtitlán. When the Spaniards came in 1519, it was the beginning of the end for the Aztecs. By 1521, they had been conquered. Mexico City was built on the ruins of Tenochtitlán.

Awesome! Now that you've read about the Mayans, Incas, and Aztecs, you may want to read about the history of the Mayan Empire in the Baby Professor book The History of the Mayan Empire

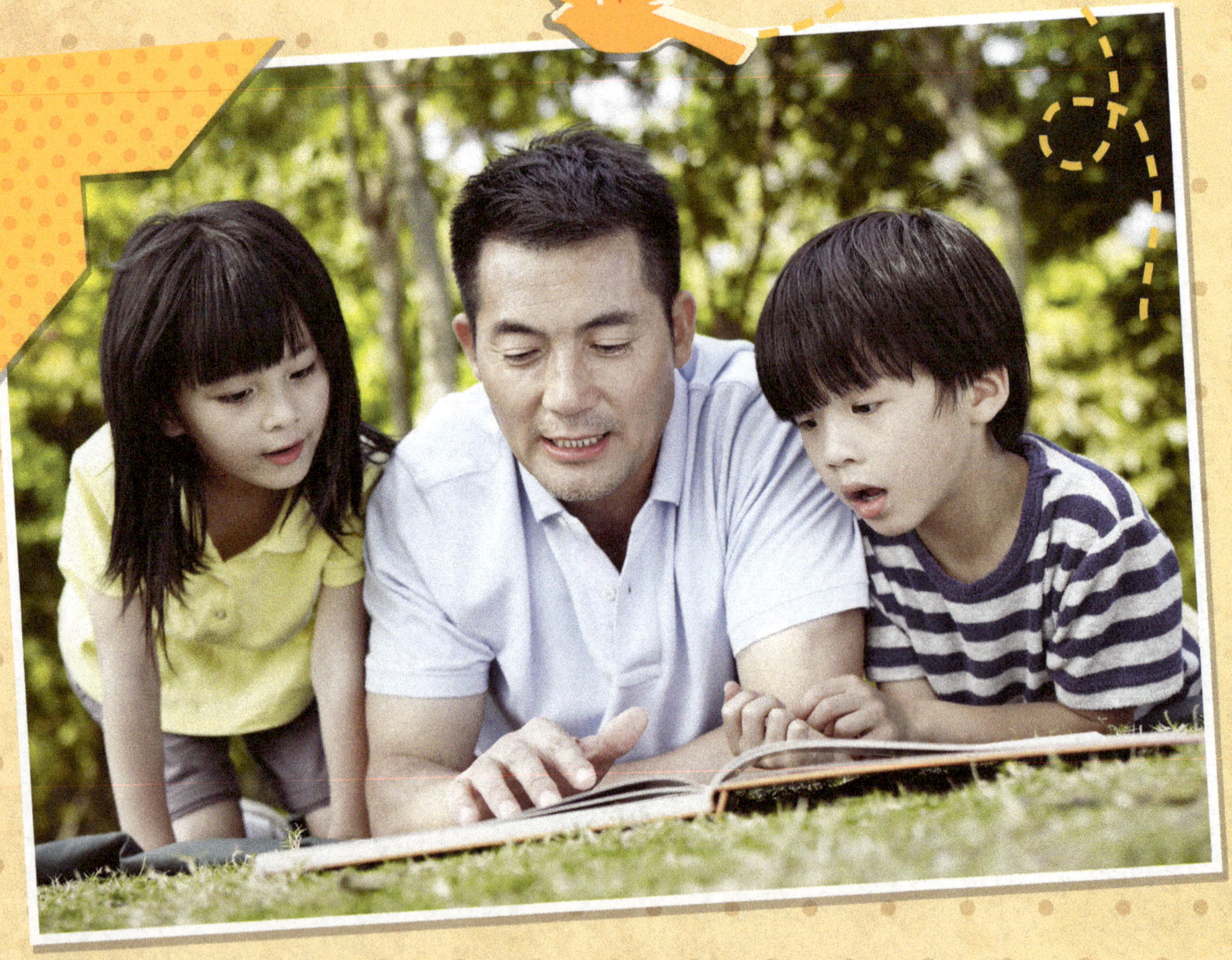

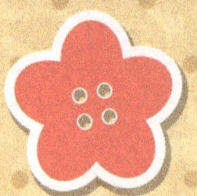

Visit

BABY PROFESSOR
EDUCATION KIDS

www.BabyProfessorBooks.com

to download Free Baby Professor eBooks
and view our catalog of new and exciting
Children's Books